FLYING THE E-Jet

The basics of flying Embraer's E-Jet family of commercial airliners

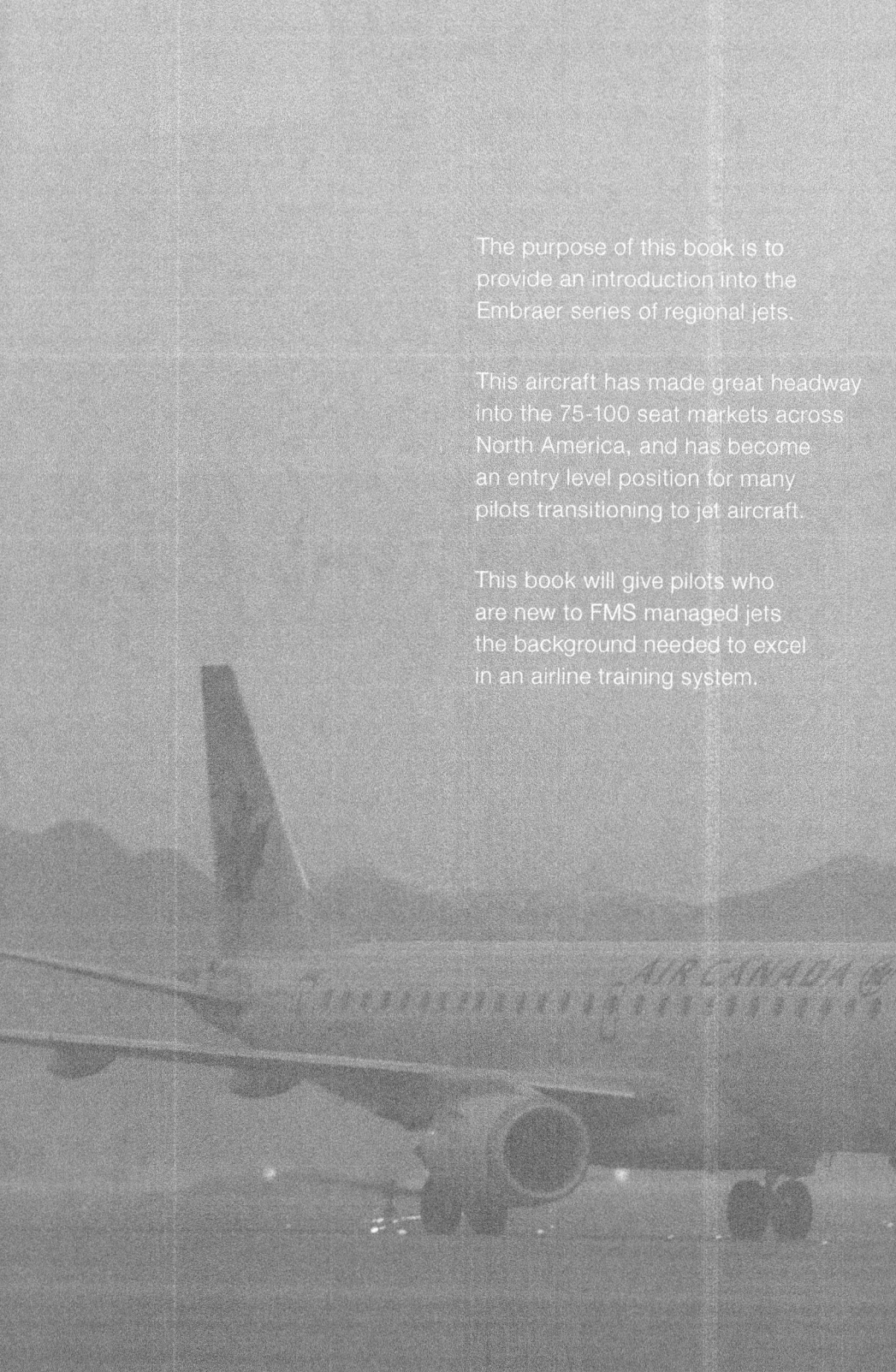

The purpose of this book is to
provide an introduction into the
Embraer series of regional jets.

This aircraft has made great headway
into the 75-100 seat markets across
North America, and has become
an entry level position for many
pilots transitioning to jet aircraft.

This book will give pilots who
are new to FMS managed jets
the background needed to excel
in an airline training system.

INTRODUCTION TO THE E-JET

SYSTEMS

EXTERIOR   **62**

01_

INTRODUCTION TO THE E-JET

HISTORY OF THE E JET

The E-Jet was developed in 2002 in response to industry demands for more efficient, flexible aircraft with 70 to 120 seat capacity. The Embraer E-Jet was designed from the ground-up, not a stretch version of an existing aircraft. This design allowed for optimal efficiency and comfort for the target market.

By January 2014 over 1000 E-Jets had been delivered worldwide.

The interior of the E-Jet is favoured by many passengers as it offers a 2 and 2 configuration, eliminating the middle seat.

A GREENER JET

The E-Jet is a greener jet than most others in its class, producing 50% less Carbon Dioxide than older jets of similar size such as the DC9, MD87 and early 737 models.

FOR PILOTS NEW TO JETS

A REVIEW OF INERTIA

Pilots currently flying medium turboprop aircraft are likely accustomed to flying around at 250 knots, with a mass of 9000 kg. These aircraft have inertia of about 1,000,000 Newtons. The basic principles are the same when flying larger jet aircraft, however the inertia is much greater. Average medium jets– like the E-Jet– weigh about 45,000 kgs and cruise at 450 knots. That is approximately ten times the inertia of lighter, turbo-prop aircraft. This means in order to stay ahead of the aircraft pilots need to think further ahead in all phases of flight.

ENGINE SPOOL UP TIME

Modern turbofan engines take much longer to develop full thrust than the propeller counterparts. Engines at idle will take 8 to 10 seconds to develop maximum rated thrust, so pilots need to be ready to make large adjustments well in advance of when thrust increases are needed.

Thrust is exponentially related to the thrust lever angle: 90% of the thrust is made in the top 10 % of the thrust lever movement. Pilots should be sensitive to this when adjusting thrust in this range.

MODEL VARIANTS

Five model variants have been produced to date:

+ Embraer 170 & Embraer 175

The E170 and E175 both use the General Electric CF34 - 8E power plant to develop 13800 lbs of thrust. The E170 is designed for 78 passengers and the E175 is designed for 86 passengers.

+ Embraer 190 & Embraer 195

The larger variants of the E-Jet use the General Electric CF-34 -10E power plant, producing 18500 lbs of thrust. Passenger capacity is 106 and 118 for the E190 and E195 respectively.

+ Lineage 1000

This is a business jet version of the E190 offering up to 4200 nm range to compete with other large business jets.

Most countries have adopted a common type endorsement for all variants of the aircraft.

+ E2 Family

The next generation of the Embraer E-Jet family was launched at the Paris Air Show in 2013, Embraer E-Jets E2 are scheduled for first deliveries in 2018.

01_

An E170 operated by Alitalia Express

Andrea Graziano, Creative Commons

An E170 operated by LOT

Marcin Jagodziński, Creative Commons

An E190 operated by Finnair

Chris Eisenbahner, Creative Commons

An E195 operated by Air Europa

Humphrey Manusiwa, Creative Commons

01_

The Lineage business jet variant based
on the E190

Noel Jones, Creative Commons

The Lineage interior

Jetrequest.com, Creative Commons

The flight deck is standardized across
the E-Jet family

Sergey Ryabtsev, Creative Commons

Commercial E-Jet interior

MarinaSilva, Creative Commons

01_

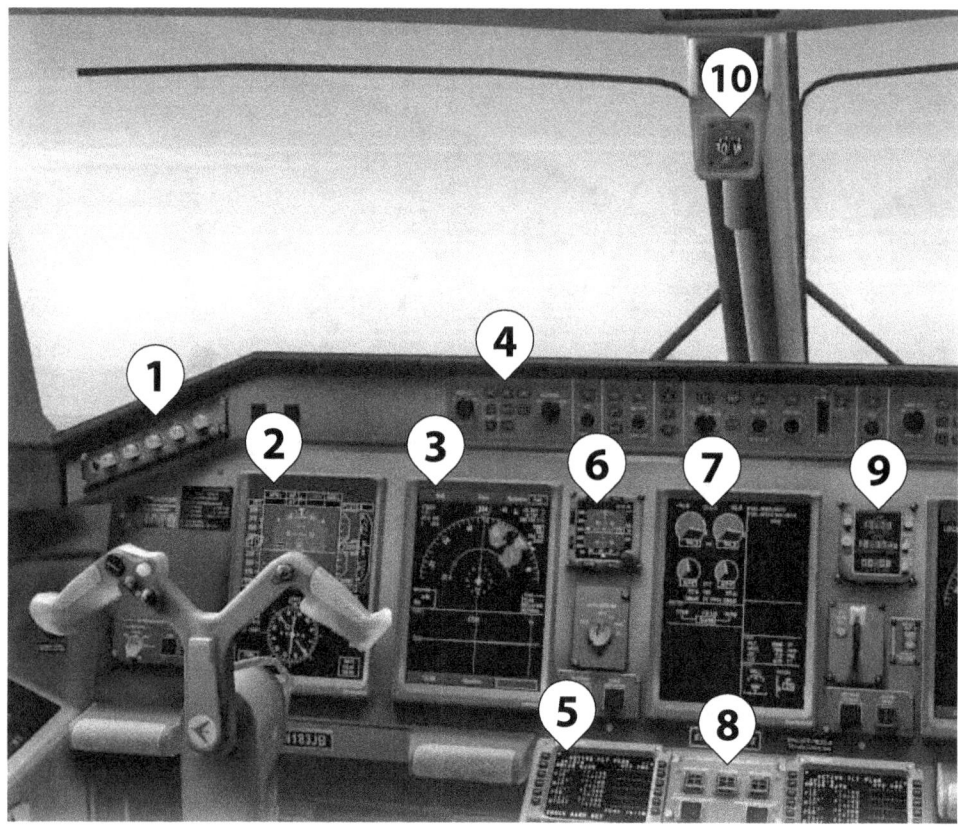

FLIGHT DECK OVERVIEW

On initial glance at the flight deck of the Embraer, pilots will notice five large liquid crystal displays, and relatively few controls on the main panel. The flight deck has two control columns which have an "M" shape control wheel: an ergonomic design that allows comfortable hand flying for extended periods.

01_

Guidance Panel

THE GUIDANCE PANEL

The guidance panel allows the pilots to interact with the aircraft flight control and instrumentation systems. Flight modes are selected on the guidance panel and cross checked with the Primary Flight Display (PFD).

PRIMARY FLIGHT DISPLAY

01_ Airspveed Indicator

The airspeed tape is located on the left side of the PFD and has overlays of different colours and letters.

02_ Low Speed Awareness Bands

The red band represents the shaker speed where the stick shaker will activate.

The yellow band represents 1.13 of Vs in the current configuration.

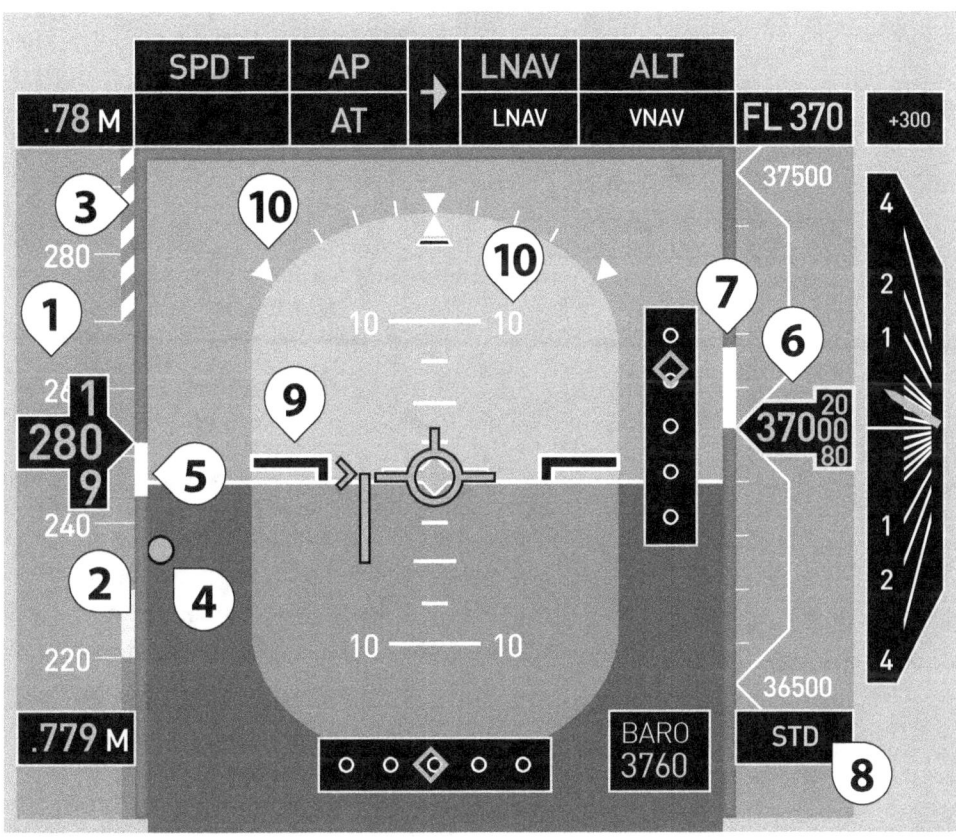

Primary Flight Display

Both the speed tapes are continually updated to reflect weight and load factor.

03_ Barber Pole

Red and white striped tape displays Vmo or Mmo, corrected for altitude.

04_ Green Dot

The green dot floats to the right of the airspeed tape and displays the drift down speed or, if flaps are extended, the flap maneuvering speed.

01_

05_ Speed Trend

A white bar varies in magnitude directly with the acceleration and deceleration rate. The end of the trend bar represents the predicted airspeed in 10 seconds.

06_ Altimeter Indications

The altitude tape is portrayed on the right side of the PFD.

07_ Altitude Trend

The trend bar displays the predicted altitude in 6 seconds.

08_ Altimeter settings

The barometric altimeter setting and units are displayed in cyan at the bottom of the altimeter tape. Inches of Hg or hPa are selected on the guidance panel. STD is displayed when the standard selection is active

09_ ADI Display

Attitude indications are displayed by 2 black wings and 1 black square representing the nose relative to the horizon.

10_ Pitch and Roll Indices

Pitch is displayed in degrees above and below the horizon in increments of 2.5 degrees. Bank is indicated with lines at 10, 20 30 and 60 degrees with Inverted triangles at 45 degrees.

Above 25000 feet ASL and in heading mode a bank limit is overlaid at the top of the ADI. The reduced bank limit is 18 degrees left and right. This mode is also activated anytime by the pilots selecting BANK mode on the guidance panel.

FLIGHT PATH VECTOR - FPV

The flight path vector represents the actual path of the aircraft. When attitude changes are occurring, like during a go- around, the FPV and the position of the nose and wings will not be overlapping. The flight director will display guidance in the form of a magenta diamond, which pilots will follow with the green FPV.

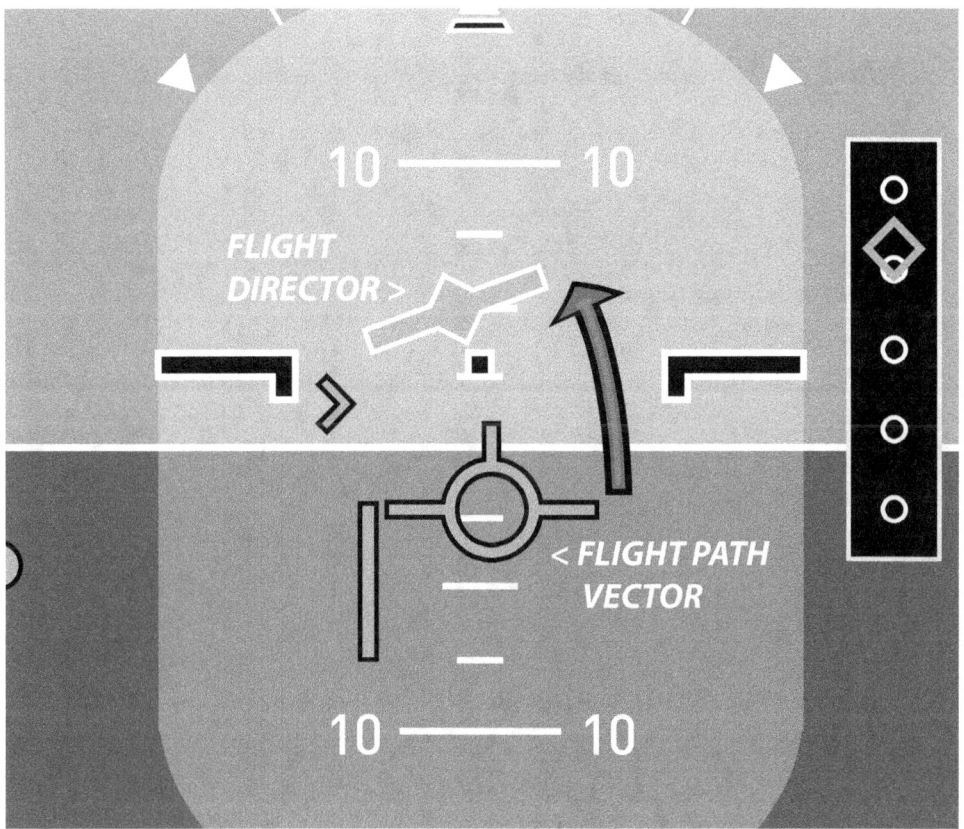

Flight Path Vector during a go-around

▼ SPEED ERROR

Any difference between the selected or commanded speed and the current speed will be displayed to the left of the FPV, in the form of a tape, similar to the speed trend. It is displayed closer to the centre of the PFD for ease of scan and information processing by the pilot.

The size of the tape varies directly with the amount of speed error. When the error is below the "wing" of the FPV, the speed is currently less than selected, and vice versa when the error is above the wing.

01_

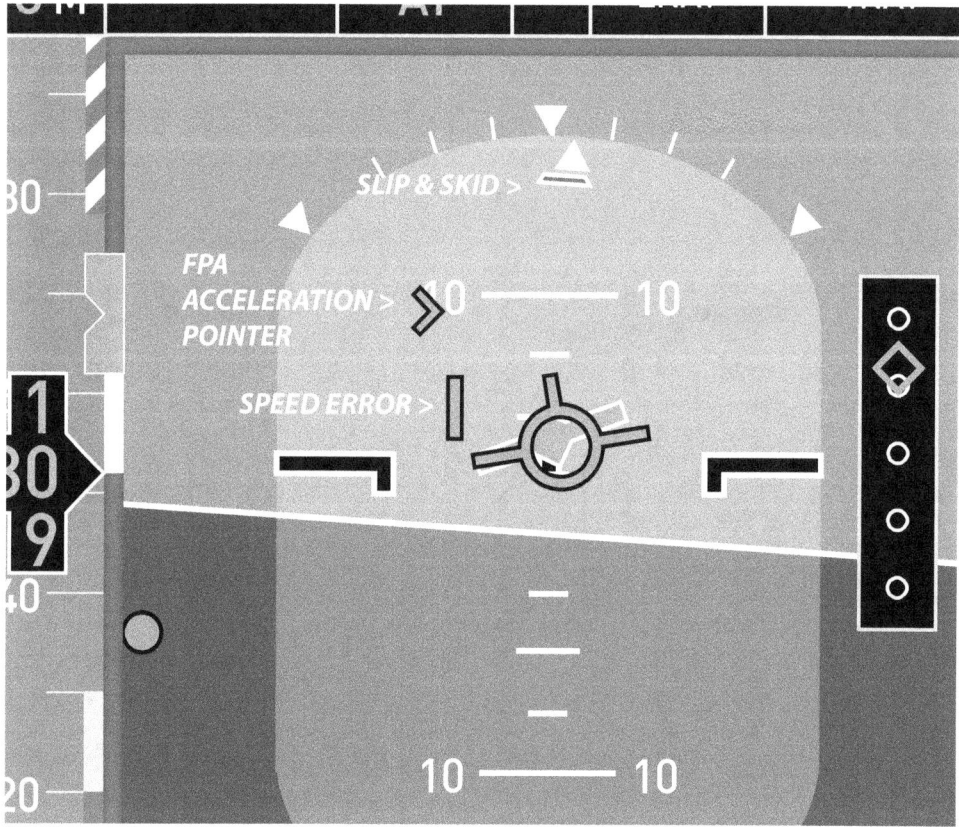

Speed error and acceleration pointer in a turning climb

▶ FLIGHT PATH ANGLE ACCELERATION POINTER

A chevron to the left of the FPV provides indication of accelerations and decelerations of the flight path. Since the pointer is a vector it is a better indication of energy management than solely using the airspeed trend.

If the FPV is accelerating, or the aircraft is gaining energy, the chevron moves above the wing. Similarly, when decelerating the chevron is below the wing. This can be seen clearly when the aircraft is flying through windshear or mountain wave: the aircraft loses and gains energy before the airspeed, altimeter or thrust can respond.

▶ SLIP AND SKID

Coordination is represented by a black bar that slides to the left and right of the white triangle. In normal flight conditions the bar is evenly under the triangle.

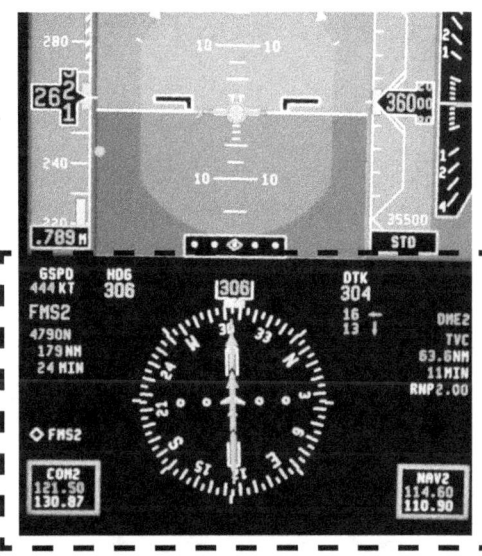

The boxed-in area shows the Horizontal Situation Indicator

HORIZONTAL SITUATION INDICATOR (HSI)

The Horizontal Situation Indicator incorporates the following data into its display:

Nav Source

Active to Waypoint - "X" prefix means navigating to an "abeam" fix

Com 1 or 2 Active and Standby

Nav 1 or 2 Active and Standby

DME 1 or 2, Identifier, Distance, Time

RNP level

Wind (in Vector mode)

Preview Pointer

Preview identifier - currently FMS 1 bearing pointer

01_

MULTIFUNCTION DISPLAY (MFD)

The Multifunction Display can present either navigation or systems information. The pilot selects the desired pages using the Cursor Control Device (CCD) mounted on the center pedestal.

▼ MAP PAGE

Navigation Source

Air Data and Wind Vector

Terrain information - EGPWS

TCAS settings

Flight Progress information

Navaids and Airports can be overlaid to the Map and Plan pages for

The map display as shown on the MFD, also shows terrain and TCAS targets

situational awareness. Navaids are shown in green and airports are cyan.

Predicted Track lines are shown on the MFD and PFD as the white triangle at the top of the compass rose. Here the aircraft is heading 260, but the track over the ground is around 269, overlapping on the magenta track, which is the FMS desired track. More crosswind, the more of a split between the PTL and the current heading

▼ PLAN PAGE

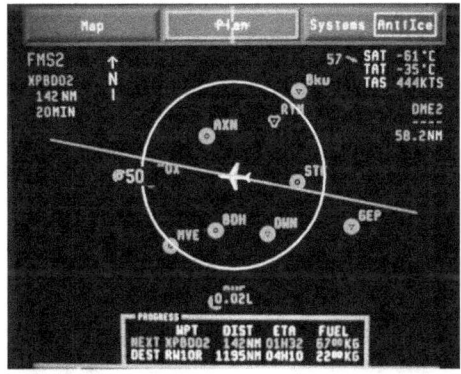

The plan page presents similar information as the map page, except in a "North-Up" orientation, 360 degrees around the aircraft. The plan page can be selected to aircraft centered or waypoint centered.

Scale is changed using the cursor control device rotating knob.

When on Waypoint center, the pilot can scroll through waypoints and the vertical profile will also scroll, showing any constraints built into the active vertical flight plan.

▼ VERTICAL PROFILE

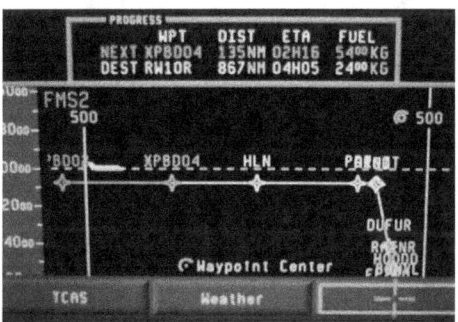

Below the Map, Plan and Systems pages a vertical profile can be selected, which shows the aircraft's planned descent and altitude constraints.

▼ MFD - SYSTEMS PAGES

Systems pages show pertinent information about the aircraft systems

01_

Status Page

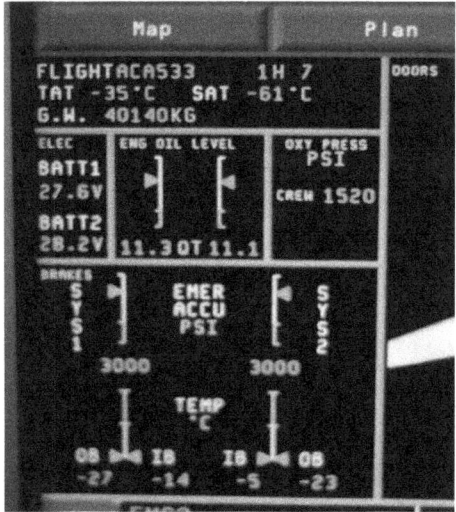

Flight Controls

Hydraulic

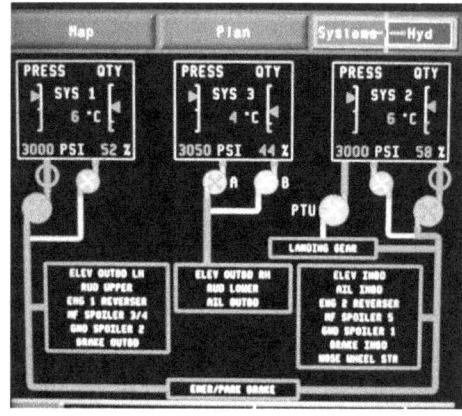

Fuel

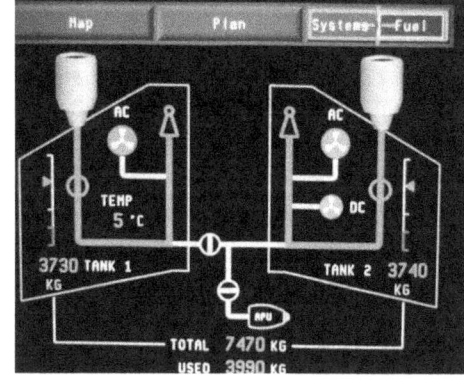

Electrical

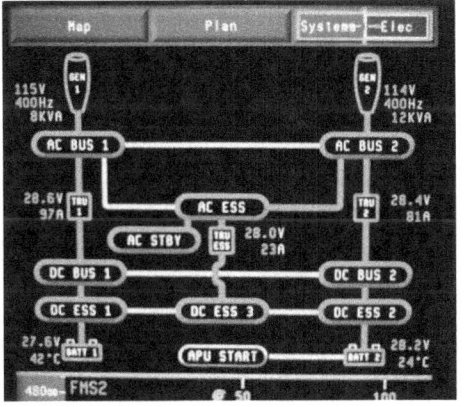

Anti Ice

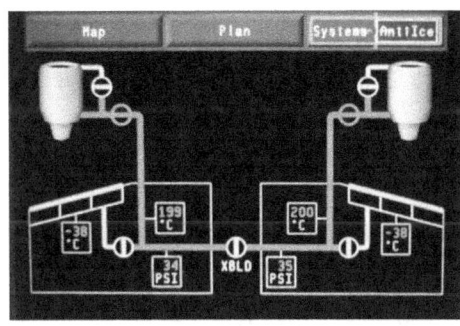

Environmental Controls - ECS

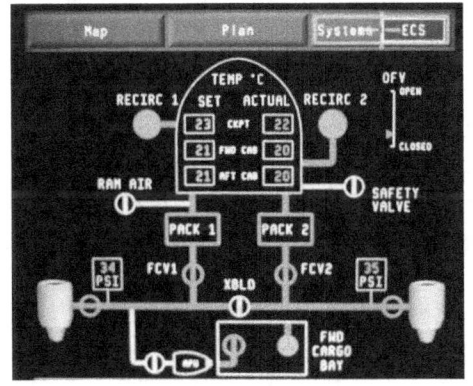

TCAS MENU

A TCAS display can be shown on any of the navigation or systems displays. Relative altitudes of nearby targets are shown, and absolute altitudes (ASL) can also be shown by selecting ABS. The TCAS range ring is controlled by CCD

01_

Normal: +/-2700 feet

Above: +9900 to - 2700 feet

Below: +2700 to - 9900 feet

Expanded: +/- 9900 feet.

range scales, EICAS lists and radio frequencies.

CURSOR CONTROL DEVICE (CCD)

Each pilot has a cursor control device to interact with the aircraft EFIS displays. Located on the centre pedestal abeam the pilots inboard knee, the CCD is very easy to use and works similar to a touch pad on a laptop. The CCD has 2 selector buttons (like a mouse button) and 3 display selectors. The display selectors represent the PFD, MFD and EICAS display for each pilot. The default position is on the MFD as the majority of interaction occurs with that screen during normal operation.

The rotating knob of the CCD provides the interaction with

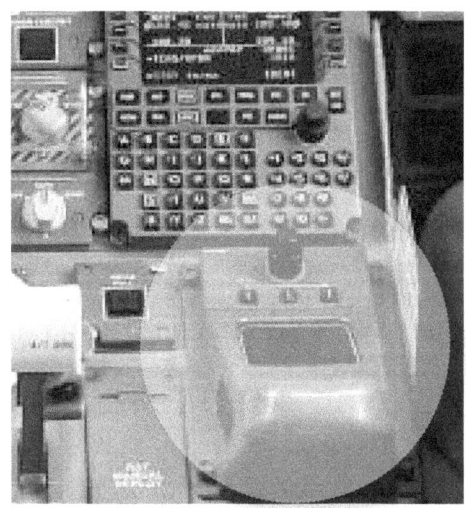

Right side Cursor Control Device

02_

SYSTEMS

POWER PLANT

The Embraer is powered by two high bypass twin spool turbofan engines.

The engines are controlled through a FADEC system, each with 2 channels for redundancy. Each channel is identical but only one channel is active at a time, the inoperative channel acts as a standby, continually processing and checking the controls of the active channel, if required the standby channel will activate to assume control of the system.

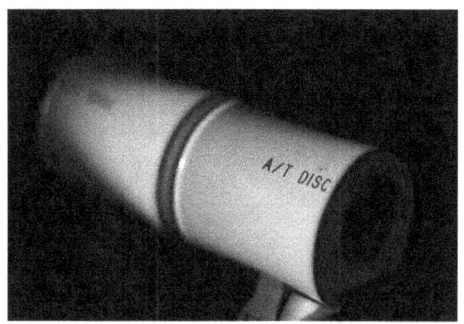

Thrust levers and Auto Throttle Disconnect buttons

FADEC: FULL AUTHORITY DIGITAL ENGINE CONTROL

A computer controls engine parameters to achieve the performance desired by the pilot. FADEC eases much of the workload associated with turbine engines as it allows pilots to set thrust for a given phase of flight and the FADEC will control the engine within its parameters. FADEC controls the engine from start to shutdown during normal and abnormal conditions.

DE-RATES AND FLEX

Turbofan engines are very reliable and rarely suffer failures. Statistically, when the turbojet or turbofan engine fails , it usually occurs during thrust changes. In order to reduce the frequency of engine failures and to reduce maintenance costs the Embraer E-Jet uses thrust derates and flex temperatures to optimize the balance between performance and cost efficiency.

Thrust **de-rates** limit the maximum thrust produced by the engine. The Embraer uses two de-rates to limit thrust from the maximum value of Takeoff 1 (TO-1). The de-rates are known as Takeoff - 2 (TO-2), and Takeoff -3 (TO-3).

Flex will further allow a thrust reduction by calculating takeoff performance using an assumed temperature. By "flexing" the takeoff the takeoff performance at the current temperature is known, then it is calculated at 1 degree increments until the value is found that will not allow a takeoff from that runway, when other atmospheric conditions remain constant. For each degree that the temperature increases the maximum allowable thrust and therefore, N1 speed decreases.

The **flex** temperature value is entered into the MCDU before takeoff and the flex temperature value is displayed on the EICAS during the takeoff.

▼ EXAMPLE

✈ Actual temperature is 19 C

✈ Under the current conditions the crew determines that the flex temperature is 43 C

✈ 43 C is entered into the MCDU before engine start.

✈ On takeoff the engine will limit itself to an ITT as if it was actually 43 C

✈ The aircraft departs using the optimum balance of thrust reduction for that specific runway.

In reality, the aircraft performs better than the published performance as the real temperature is only 19 C and factors such as TAS, and density altitude are better than calculated.

02_

THRUST RATINGS

Thrust Rating		Description
Idle	Ground Idle	Minimum idle for ground operations
	Approach Idle	Higher idle speed to provide faster engine response during a go around Flaps 1 or more and gear down Below 15000 feet
	Final Approach Idle	Higher idle speed to provide faster engine response during a low altitude Go Around Landing flaps and gear down Below 1200 feet
	Flight Idle	Min Thrust in Flight Varies with Air Density
Max Continuous	CON	Maximum thrust for continuous use. CON mode is automatically selected when an engine failure is sensed

Thrust Rating		Description
Climb	CLB 1	Upon aircraft startup the default setting is CLB 1. If the pilot selects a thrust derate for takeoff that results in a lower N_1 than rated for CLB 1, CLB 2 will now become the default.
	CLB 2	Greater derate Less thrust and fuel flow Can be up to 4% lower than CLB 1.
Cruise	CRZ	Maximum N_1 for cruise flight
Go - Around	GA	Activated with gear down, normal go around thrust
Go- Around Reserve	GA- RSV	Maximum thrust for go- arounds

The above thrust terms refer to the rating or maximum value for that given mode. The autothrust system will determine appropriate thrust to maintain speed when required.

02_

THRUST LEVERS

The thrust levers of the Embraer are simple and easy to use.

There are 5 detents:

01_ MAX

Placing the Thrust Levers over the TOGA detent will command MAX thrust from the engines for the given conditions.

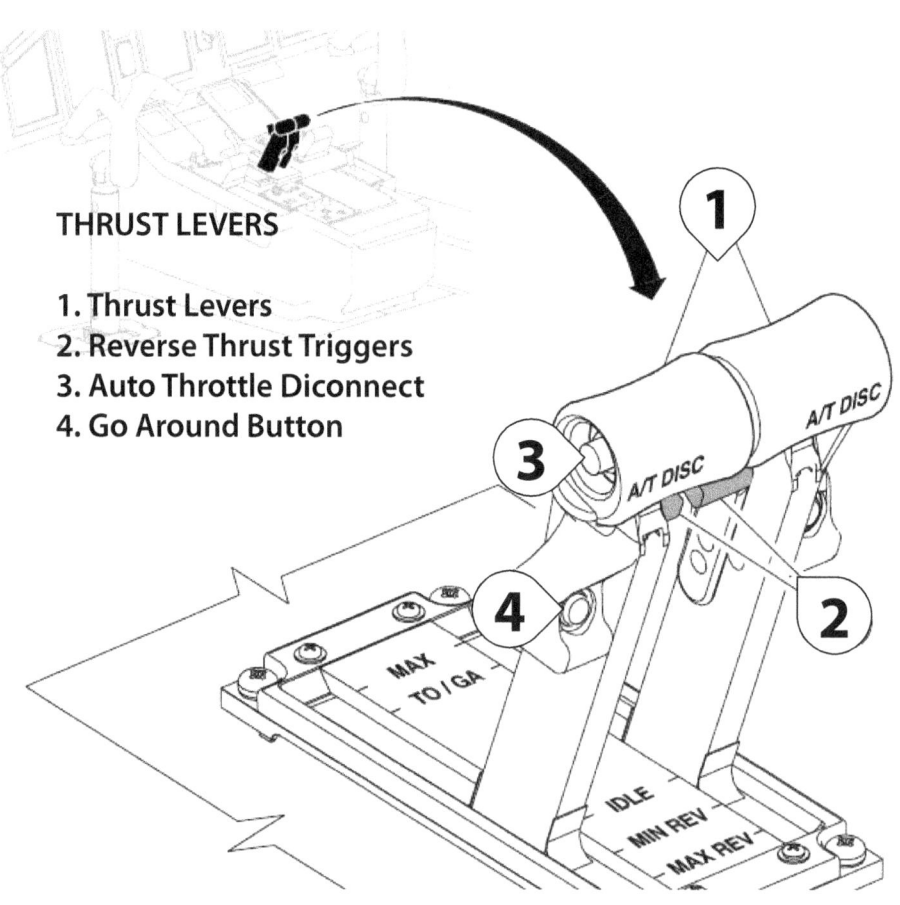

THRUST LEVERS

1. Thrust Levers
2. Reverse Thrust Triggers
3. Auto Throttle Diconnect
4. Go Around Button

02_ TO/GA

At the TOGA detent the engines will produce takeoff (TO -n) Continuous (CON), or Go Around (GA) thrust.

03_ IDLE

Pulling the thrust lever back to the idle detent will command flight, ground, approach or final approach idle speed, dependent on conditions.

04_ MIN REV

Once on the ground, pulling the 2 triggers between the thrust levers allow the selection of reverse thrust.

Pulling the levers to MIN REV opens the reversers.

05_ MAX REV

This selection commands maximum reverse thrust. As with all aerodynamic braking, it is most effective at high speeds. If reverse thrust is to be used, it should be commanded early in the landing roll.

TAKE OFF THRUST

Take off thrust reduced by:

▶ TAKEOFF 1 (TO-1)

Highest available thrust

▶ TAKEOFF 2 (TO-2) & TAKEOFF 3 (TO-3)

Flex fine tunes the thrust reduction for specific airport and atmospheric conditions. The maximum reduction of thrust is TO- 3 and Flex. The maximum flex reduction is limited by the climb thrust rating.

Reduced thrust takeoffs are used for almost all takeoffs. The minimum thrust that will be used will be 75% of the maximum thrust for the given conditions.

When takeoff thrust is reduced below the Climb -1 thrust rating, the Climb 2 thrust value will become the default for climbs for that flight, and all subsequent flights until the aircraft electrically powers down.

02_

ATTCS - AUTOMATIC TAKEOFF THRUST CONTROL SYSTEM

ATTCS is an automatic function that provides an increase in thrust in the event of an engine failure on takeoff or go-around, or a windshear encounter.

ATTCS will command Reserve (RSV) thrust when the following occurs:

→ Thrust levers at TO/GA detent

→ Thrust difference greater than 15% N1 between engines

→ Engine failure, or

→ Windshear encounter

AUTO THRUST

Auto thrust is normally engaged from runway lineup to runway exit after landing.

Once armed, Autothrust will activate when the pilot moves the thrust levers forward on takeoff.

The thrust levers move in response to FADEC engine commands but pilots can override the auto thrust at any time.

If the pilot disconnects the auto thrust in flight, an aural warning of "throttle, throttle" is given.

EICAS Display shows ATTCS, Takeoff 2, and assumed temp of 39

AUTOTHRUST MODES

Mode	FMA	Description
Speed on Thrust	SpdT	Speed control is achieved by increase and decrease of thrust
Speed on Elevator	SpdE	Speed control is achieved by Elevator (PITCH) command
Takeoff	TO	Armed on the ground before takeoff, and engages 50 degrees TLA (Thrust Lever Angle)
Takeoff Thrust Hold	HOLD	Active between 60 KIAS on takeoff to 400 ft AGL, this mode maintains takeoff thrust and prevents other thrust lever commands
Go Around	GA	Thrust levers move to TO/GA position, GA rated thrust is commanded.
Retard	RETD	Commands thrust levers to idle at 30 feet during landing flare. Idle thrust should be achieved at touchdown
Limit	LIM	The autothrust cannot maintain the selected speed.

This can occur during a descent, or during a climb in SpdT modes. |
| Override | OVRD | The pilot is overriding the TMS (Thrust Management System) command. |

02_

Autothrust is normally armed at line-up (photo: RHL Images)

FLIGHT DIRECTOR

The flight director guidance is presented to the pilot on the PFD. The current mode of the guidance system will determine which type of display the pilot sees. The flight director crossbar display is used during takeoff and during go around modes.

▼ CROSSBAR DISPLAY

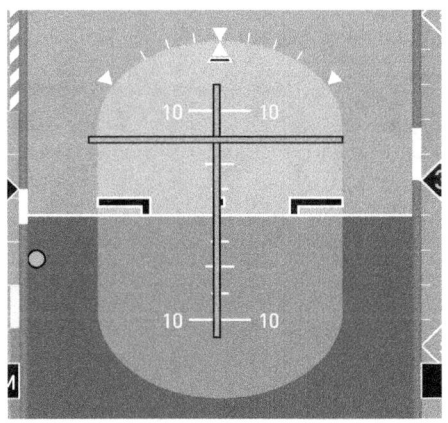

▼ DIAMOND DISPLAY

The flight director will automatically be displayed when:

✧ Windshear is encountered; or

✧ any lateral or vertical flight guidance modes are selected; or

✧ autopilot is engaged; or

✧ TO/GA button is pressed and no other mode displayed.

AUTOFLIGHT

The autoflight system uses a number of different lateral and vertical modes to control the aircraft from initial climb to decision altitude.

Mode awareness is a critical element in maintaining technical situational awareness when flying an autopilot

02_

equipped aircraft. Autoflight is controlled through the manipulation of the guidance panel (GP) located on the glare shield and monitored by the Flight Management Annunciator (FMA) at the top of the PFD.

Pilots should be aware of:

→ Current mode and next anticipated mode

→ Capabilities and limitations of current mode

→ Current autoflight performance relative to desired performance

→ Position using all available means

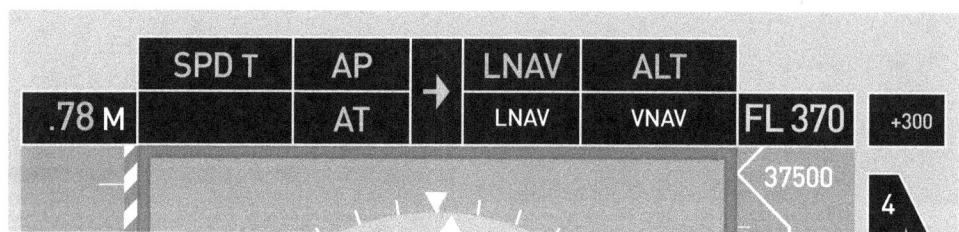

FMA Displays the auto throttle and autopilot are engaged

AUTOFLIGHT LATERAL MODES

Mode	FMA	Description
Track Hold	**TRACK**	Maintains the current aircraft track. This mode becomes active on the takeoff roll. Current aircraft track is always displayed on the MFD and PFD as a white triangle on the top of the compass rose
Roll Hold	**ROLL**	Maintains wings level attitude. Reversionary mode If LNAV is lost, or selected off.
Heading Select	**HDG**	Turns to and maintains the pilot selected heading. Above 25000 feet the heading mode reduces bank commands to 18 degrees to minimize cruise load factors. Since the heading selector is pilot controlled, it is cyan in colour
Localizer	**LOC**	Intercepts and tracks the localizer. Green display as it is derived from a ground based nav- aid.
Back Course	**BC**	Intercepts and tracks back course approaches. Green display as it is derived from a ground based nav- aid.
Lateral Nav	**LNAV**	Magenta FMA, as it is FMS derived.

02_

AUTOFLIGHT VERTICAL MODES

Mode	FMA	Description
Flight Path Angle	**FPA**	A mode to fly a constant flight path. For example, 1.5 degrees nose down could be maintained with this mode Speed is controlled by thrust in this mode
Takeoff	**TO**	Displays command bars for V2 +10 knots target, based on entered speeds and aircraft mass. Lateral path displayed is track, which activates at 100 knots during takeoff.
Flight Level Change	**FLCH**	Flight Level Change maintains speed control through the elevator, and will command either Climb thrust, when below the selected altitude, or Flight Idle thrust when above the selected altitude.
Altitude Hold	**ALT**	Maintains the selected altitude
Altitude Select	**ASEL**	Captures selected altitude, not selected by the pilot. Speed is controlled by thrust in this mode
Glideslope	**GS**	Controls autoflight to maintain ILS Glideslope. Speed is controlled by thrust in this mode
VNAV Glidepath	**VGP**	Controls autoflight to maintain FMS managed Glidepath. Speed is controlled by thrust in this mode

Go Around	GA	Pitch command to Vref +20 (2 engines) or Vac (1 engine).
		GA mode remains engaged until another vertical mode is selected.
		Speed is controlled by elevator in this mode

FMA MODES DURING FLIGHT

▶ TAKEOFF

After loading takeoff performance pilots can push the TOGA button on either thrust lever, which arms the takeoff mode, and displays the flight director guidance on each PFD.

The FMA will show ROLL, and TO armed in white.

Turning onto the active runway pilots normally arm the auto thrust system.

While advancing the thrust levers during the takeoff the auto thrust activates and the thrust levers move on their own to the TOGA detent.

At 100 knots during takeoff the roll turns to TRACK and the aircraft maintains the current track on the runway.

▶ TOCA

At TOCA pilots normally activate the FLCH mode and activate the autopilot.

Upon the engagement of the FLCH mode the thrust rating changes to climb from the takeoff setting, and the speed is now controlled by elevator. The flight director bars change to the magenta diamond and commands an acceleration.

02_

▼ AFTER FLAP RETRACTION

FMS speed will change the speed to magenta, and command the speed to the values programmed before departure.

As a default the Embraer has a speed restriction of 250 KIAS below 10000 feet ASL.

▼ TOP OF CLIMB (TOC)

Once reaching the altitude as set in the Perf Init page, the aircraft accelerates to cruise mach. Once cruise speed is achieved then the thrust rating reverts to CRZ rating.

▼ CRUISE

During cruise the FMS will command roll rates up to 15 degrees to maintain track and maintains speed by thrust.

If heading mode is selected above 25 000 a bank limit indicator is shown on the ADI, to limit pilot induced load factor.

▼ TOP OF DESCENT (TOD)

At 200 miles to fly to destination the MCDU will prompt the pilots to enter landing data into the perf landing pages. After reviewing the STAR, and approach, pilots will load or verify any constraints to the vertical flight plan. The initial rate of descent will be displayed on progress pages. At one minute to fly until the Top of Descent (TOD) a VTA Vertical Track Annunciator will sound. ALT will change to PTH once the vertical track is intercepted and the aircraft will maintain the path, provided VNAV is selected.

▼ APPROACH

Once the aircraft is within the terminal area the FMS will autotune the ILS frequency if an ILS is selected as the approach in the active flight plan and autotune has been selected.

The ILS track can be previewed using the PREV button on the DCP (display control panel. The track should match the ILS inbound track.

Once on an intercept heading pilots can select the APP or approach mode, and the LOC and GS will be displayed in white on the FMA. Upon capture of the localizer the FMA will display LOC and the needle display on the HSI will turn green. Upon glideslope intercept, the GS will go from white to green on the FMA. Gear deployment will switch the thrust rating from cruise to go - around (GA).

LANDING

At "200" feet the aircraft makes auto callout and will call 'Approaching Minimums" at 80 feet above baro or RA minimums, then "Minimums" at the bugged minima.

At 50 feet the retard (RETD) mode arms and the when the aircraft reaches 30 feet on the radar altimeter, it will smoothly reduce the thrust to idle.

TOUCHDOWN

Upon touchdown, the flight crew will deploy thrust reverse, and the reversers will deploy and show a green REV under each engine icon.

Reverse is normally cancelled at 70 KIAS and the reversers are stowed as the aircraft leaves the active, usually around 30 to 40 KIAS.

03_

INTERFACE

MULTIFUNCTION CONTROL DISPLAY UNIT (MCDU)

The MCDU is the way the pilot communicates to the flight management system.

Pilots enter data into the MCDU using the alphanumeric keypad for a variety of functions, including:

✧ Lateral and Vertical Navigation

✧ Takeoff and landing performance data

✧ Predictions of alternate performance – "What if" analysis

✧ Datalink communications

✧ Comm and Navigation radio interface

✧ Circuit breaker interface

✧ Thrust selection and information

▼ ALPHANUMERIC KEYPAD

Most pilots are accustomed to the qwerty keyboard that is used on just about every other computer in our lives, but the MCDU uses a different type. Adjusting to this keypad takes a bit of time and is frustrating at first, but is easily learned. Just remember the first time you sent an SMS text through your flip mobile phone. It is a similar learning curve.

▼ SCRATCH PAD

A scratch pad is just what the name implies: it is a place where pilots can enter data before entering it into a specific line, or data field.

Data entered into the scratchpad field will stay in that field until placed elsewhere or deleted.

▼ LINE SELECT KEYS- LSK

There are 6 keys on each side of the display, they are named starting at 1 at the top to 6 at the bottom, and L, indicating left, and R for the right. The top left key is 1L, and the bottom right key is 6R.

These are "soft" keys and perform different functions depending on the selected page. Everyone who has used an ATM or bank machine has soft key experience.

▼ TUNING KNOB

The tuning knob can be used whenever a numerical value has been selected. It can be used to adjust nav or comm radios and transponder codes.

FUNCTION KEYS

Twelve keys open menus to access various functions of the flight management system.

03_

▼ THE IMPORTANCE OF COLOUR

Different colours on the MCDU have different meanings. The colours are coordinated throughout the other display systems.

Colour	Meaning
Cyan (a.k.a. blue)	pilot selected, performance, environmental data
Magenta (a.k.a pink)	FMS managed or derived
Amber	caution or invalid data
Red	failures
Green	modes
White	menus and titles or armed modes

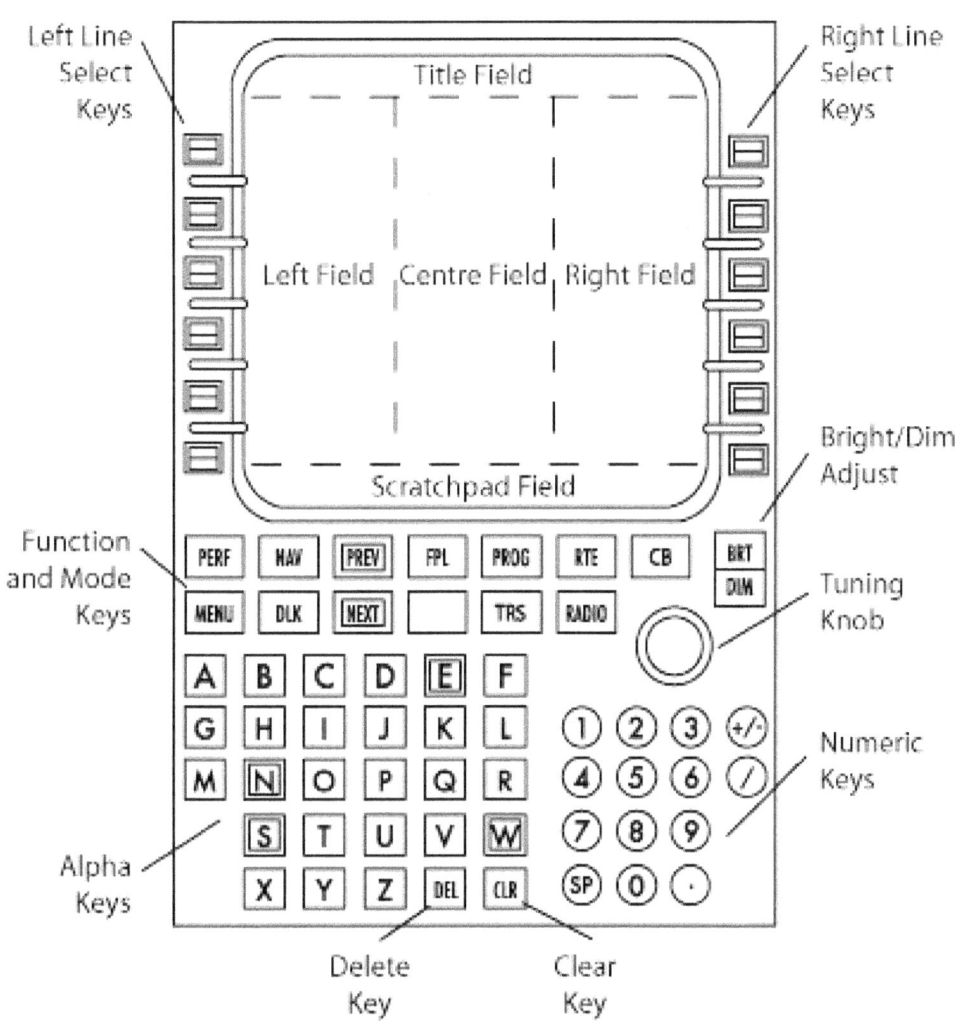

03_

▼ FUNCTION KEYS

Selecting the various function keys
open the respective menu or index.

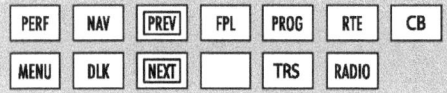

Pushing the performance key opens
the performance index page 1 of
2. Page numbers are shown in
the top right corner of the display
when there is more than 1 page.

Pushing the function key twice will
change the display to the first page
of the function. For example, if you
have Flight Plan page 5 currently
displayed, and you press the FPL
key twice, page 1 of the current
flight plan will be displayed.

▼ PAGING KEYS

The PREV or NEXT keys will
cycle through pages in the
same menu or function.

MCDU FUNCTION PAGES

▶ NAV INDEX

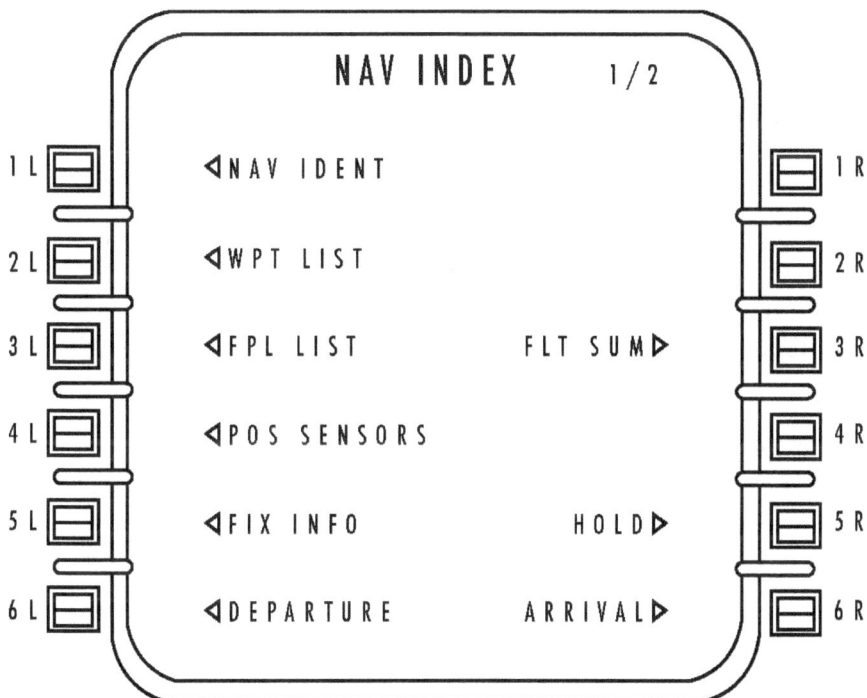

▶ NAV IDENT

This allows the pilots to view and select navigational databases and other system information.

03_

▼ WPT LIST

Displays in list format all the system defined waypoints for a active route.

Also in this page you can enter any 4 character airport code, and the system will provide you with up to 3 pages of data about that location.

▼ FPL LIST

View all the stored flight plans and select one if required from this page

▼ POS SENSORS

Displays current LAT - LONG and allows updating of the various position sensors.

Positions are displayed in order of accuracy:

FMS: The blended position of both IRS's.

IRS 1 and 2: The updated position of the respective Inertial reference system. This position is calculated at start up, then updated continually using ground based navaids and GPS.

GPS 1 and 2: position of each GPS sensor.

▼ FIX INFO

Pilots can enter fix names into this field and the fix will display on the map display, along with the bearing and distance on the MCDU.

Pilots can also enter secondary data about the fix for reference on the map display.

✧ For example:

A pilot enters CZI into the FIX INFO field.

CZI VOR is displayed on the map page with a green circle.

090 is then entered below CZI, using 2L.

the 090 Radial of CZI is
displayed ont the map page.

/18 is entered on at 3L. A ring is
drawn around CZI at 18 nm.

This feature is useful as a
backup during descent to
monitor performance.

▼ DEPARTURE

Standard instrument departures for
the departure airport are displayed
and can be selected from this
page, although activation will still
be required on the FPL page to
put the SID in the active plan.

▼ FLT SUM

Flight summary information is
provided in 3 pages. Everything from
fuel used, to air miles flown, track
miles, average TAS is available.

▼ HOLD

If there is a hold at any point in
the active flight plan it will be
displayed here. Modifications to
that hold, or entering a new hold
can be done through this page.

▼ ARRIVAL

STAR arrivals can be selected
and reviewed through this menu.
When flying a STAR via the FMS,
the FMS will create all waypoints
for that arrival routing. This way
STARs can be flown despite the
shutdown of ground based navaids.

03_

▼ USER DEFINED WAYPOINTS

Pilots can create waypoints
in the active flight plan in
the following ways:

Type	MCDU Abbreviation	MCDU Entry
Lat - long	LL## (see below)	N33W75
Place/Bearing/ Distance	PBD##	A point generated at a distance on a specific bearing. PXR/090/85 PXR VOR, 090 Radial at 85 miles.
Place/Bearing/ Place/Bearing	PBPB##	intersection of 2 radials LAX/300 and GMN/125

Lat/Long waypoints created from
the MCDU 1, or left side have odd
numbers, the right MCDU creates
even numbered waypoints.

03_

PERF INDEX

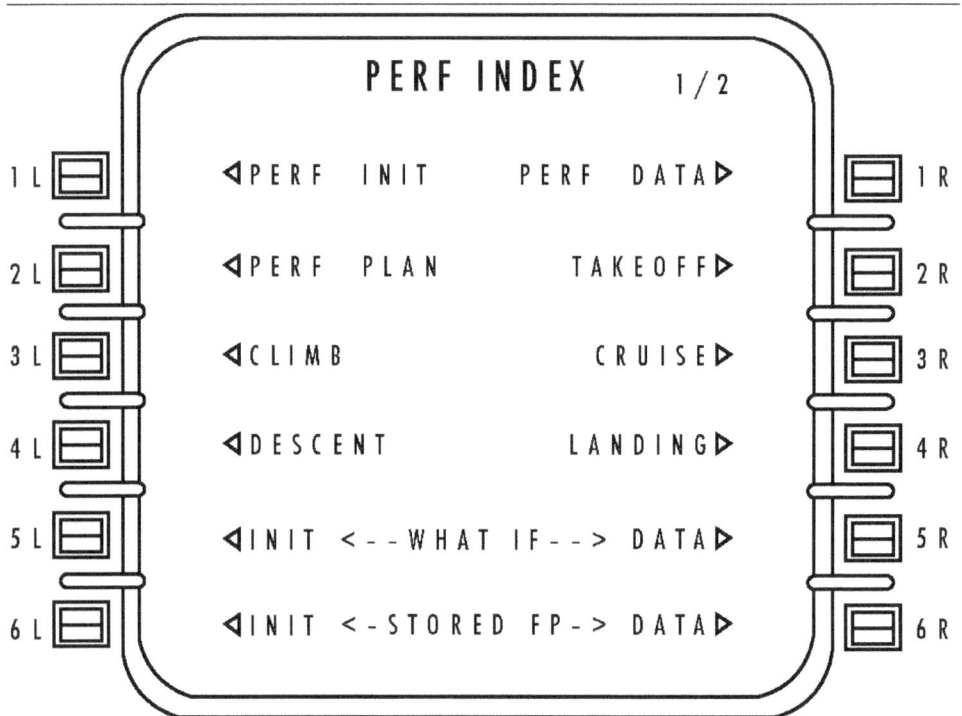

```
              PERF INDEX      1/2

1L    ◀PERF INIT        PERF DATA▶    1R

2L    ◀PERF PLAN          TAKEOFF▶    2R

3L    ◀CLIMB               CRUISE▶    3R

4L    ◀DESCENT            LANDING▶    4R

5L    ◀INIT <--WHAT IF--> DATA▶       5R

6L    ◀INIT <-STORED FP-> DATA▶       6R
```

▶ PERF INIT

Performance initialization is composed of 3 pages that will determine
many of the predictions and data for any given flight. This information
is normally loaded in the preflight phase and includes cruise
altitude,winds, zero fuel weight ISA deviation and fuel reserves.

▼ PERF PLAN

Performance plan page displays waypoints in the active route and time enroute, and fuel at each waypoint.

Perf Plan allows wind and actual temperatures to be entered into for more accurate predictions.

▼ CLIMB

Climb speeds and profile data about the initial climb are displayed under Perf- Climb.

▼ DESCENT

Descent speeds and profile data are displayed under Perf- Descent. Descent angle is entered on this page for VNAV PATH descent.

Transition speeds can be modified from the same page.

To view the initial rate of descent, pilots must review the data on the PROG page 2.

▼ PERF DATA

Performance data based on the performance initialization information, or when in flight, current sensed information.

Used for a gross error check against flight plans to verify lateral flight plans. It also provides information regarding time and fuel burn to destination and alternate airports.

▼ TAKEOFF

There are three pages where atmospheric andrunway conditions, flap setting, and takeoff speeds can be entered.

When wind is entered on the Perf -Takeoff page 1, headwind and crosswind are both displayed, relative to the runway of departure.

When entering takeoff speeds, the speed will turn inverse video (black letters on cyan background) if the speeds are out of sequence, Such as V2 slower than Vr.

03_

Takeoff speeds are also displayed on the speed tape of the PFD 1 and 2.

Once the speeds are entered, the aircraft will generate an initial pitch attitude target on takeoff. That pitch target is displayed by the flight directors once the TOGA button is pressed.

▼ CRUISE

Current cruise settings are displayed under Perf - Cruise. Along the right side of the current setting is an "OR" prompt. Pressing the prompt will allow crews to select Max Endurance, Max range and Long Range cruise settings.

This is useful if diverting to an alternate, as most times this is flight planned at max range cruise speed, cost index 0.

▼ LANDING

Through Perf - Landing pilots can enter surface conditions, and temperature corrections for the landing aerodrome.

Pilots enter Vref, Vap, Vac and Vfs for the approach.

The speed tape on the PFD also displays the Vref, and Vapp during the approach. Vac appears during the go around, as does Vfs.

On the PFD, Vf appears once the first selection of flap is made, and it represents the optimum speed to select the next flap setting.

Vf also appears on takeoffs with flap settings greater than 1. The optimum speed to retract flaps from 1 to 0 is Vfs.

▼ "WHAT IF" CALCULATIONS

The MCDU can allow an alternate performance calculations to be entered for crews to assess how it would affect the flight.

▼ EO RANGE

Engine out range is displayed during one engine inoperative flight to provide information regarding engine out cruise data.

CIRCUIT BREAKER MENUS

Through this menu, crews can monitor status of circuit breakers and integrity of fuses.

When the CB function Key is selected,, the CB's that are currently out or that have been locked out (by maintenance) are displayed.

By selecting 6L, CB MENU and selecting system, or bus, all the associated controllable circuit breakers are displayed.

When an item such as the APU is inoperative and the aircraft dispatched under MEL, crews can check that the MEL has been carried out by observing circuit breaker status.

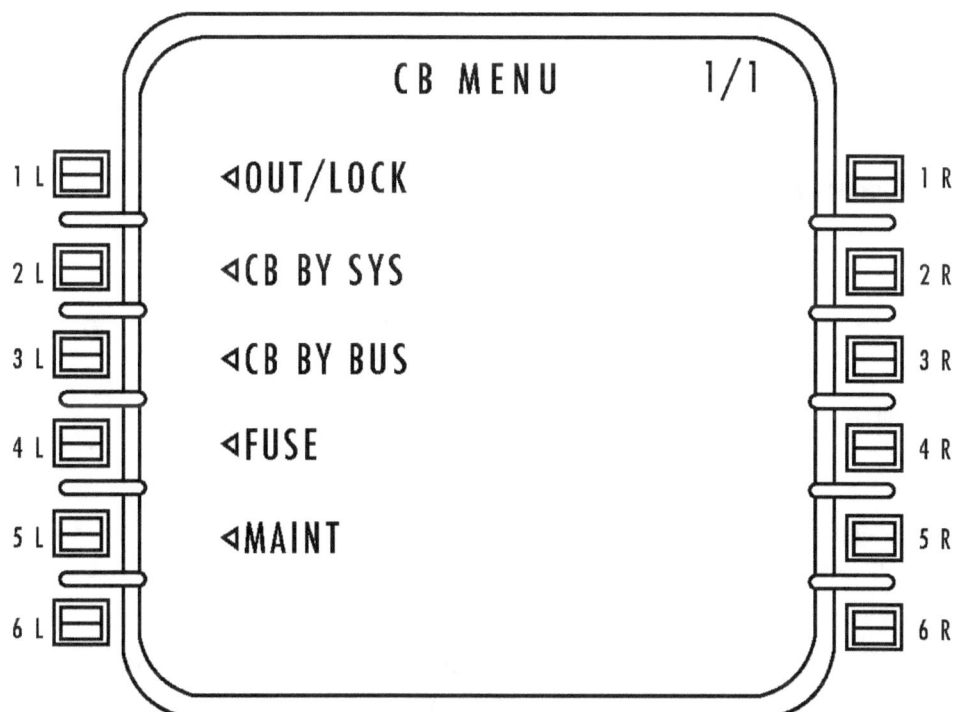

CB MENU   1/1

1 L   ◁OUT/LOCK   1 R

2 L   ◁CB BY SYS   2 R

3 L   ◁CB BY BUS   3 R

4 L   ◁FUSE   4 R

5 L   ◁MAINT   5 R

6 L   6 R

03_

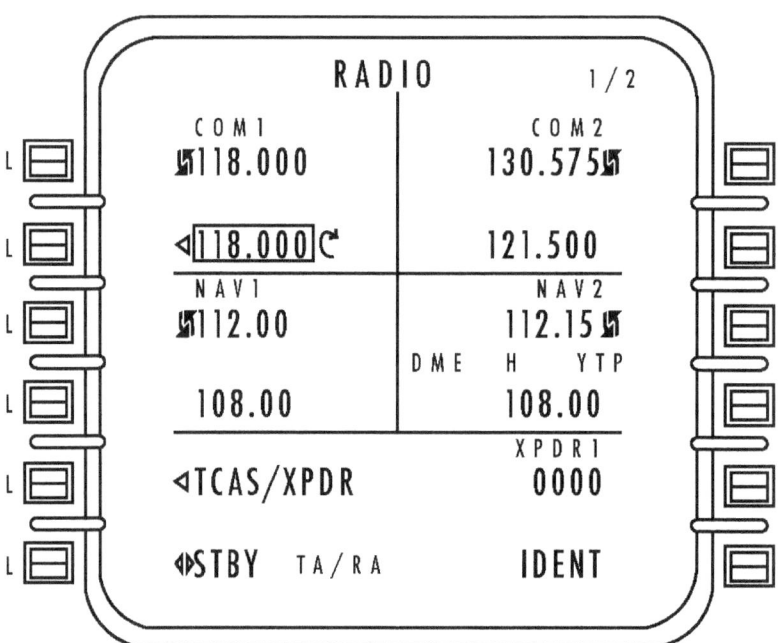

RADIO FUNCTION

Pressing the radio function key will cause page 1 of the radio menu to be displayed.

Comm and nav radios can be tuned through this page, as well as advanced functions such as DME hold, and memory recall. The transponder and TCAS level are also controlled on page 1.

▼ COMMUNICATION RADIOS

Pilots can manually select a frequency by entering the middle digits of any selectable VHF frequency. The system assumes that the first digit is a 1, and the last digit is auto-filled based on kHz spacing selection.

To tune frequency 121.50 MHz, select 215 via the keypad, and it will display in the scratch pad. Then the frequency can be placed in one of four locations, 1L for active Com 1, 1R for active Com 2, 2L for standby Com 1, and 2R for standby Com 2.

To select 130.95 MHz, 3 0 9 5 must be entered into the scratch pad.

If a com frequency value is placed into 3L, 4L, 3R or 4R, in the nav section, a message "INVALID ENTRY" will appear in the scratch pad.

An alternative method for tuning is provided through the two level knob on the MCDU.

For the tuning knob to be active, the scratch pad must be clear, and the circular arrow is displayed in the standby window of Com 1 or 2, or Nav 1 or 2.

The circular arrow is depicted at the far right of Com 1 standby at 2L. Pilots can use the large knob for whole frequencies, and small knob for fractions.

Once a nav frequency is selected or entered, the FMS AUTO function is then disabled. When this occurs it can be seen in 3 areas, Radio page 1, Prog page 1 and on each

PFD in the lower right corner. On the PFD the frequency will revert to green from magenta to indicate it is no longer managed.

▼ TRANSPONDER FUNCTION

Transponder and TCAS mode is controlled through soft key 5L, which allows the selections of TA/RA, TA only, Altitude Reporting On, or Altitude Off. Once the mode selection is made, then the STBY/TARA function is used to control the system. Active modes are displayed in larger text.

Transponder codes can be entered at 5R, and by pressing 5R twice a secondary menu opens to insert an aircraft ident, which will be displayed between 5L and 6L.

Transponder ident feature is available at 6R.

Radio page 2 displays Comm 3, which is normally used for ACARS and datalink capability.

03_

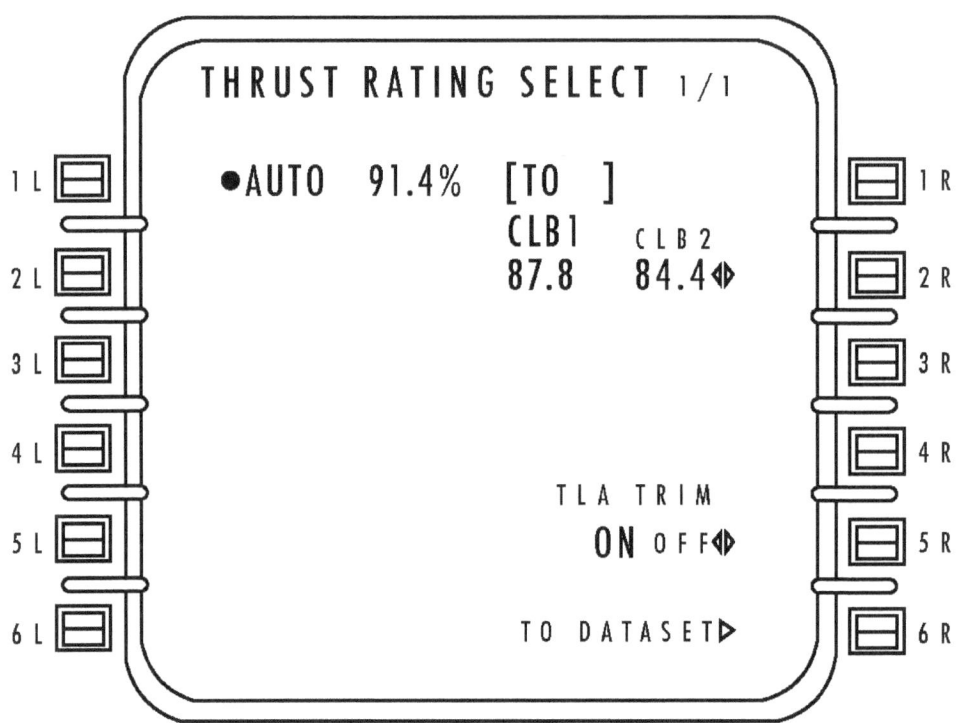

THRUST RATING SELECT (TRS)

This function allows for manual selection of a thrust rating, and offers the ability to change climb thrust between climb 1 and 2.

The takeoff data set is selected at 6R and will allow entering of

environmental and aircraft conditions to calculate the takeoff thrust target.

Auto TRS will select appropriate modes of thrust for the current phase of flight.

▶ TAKEOFF DATA SET MENU

On this page, takeoff derates, the ambient temperature, and

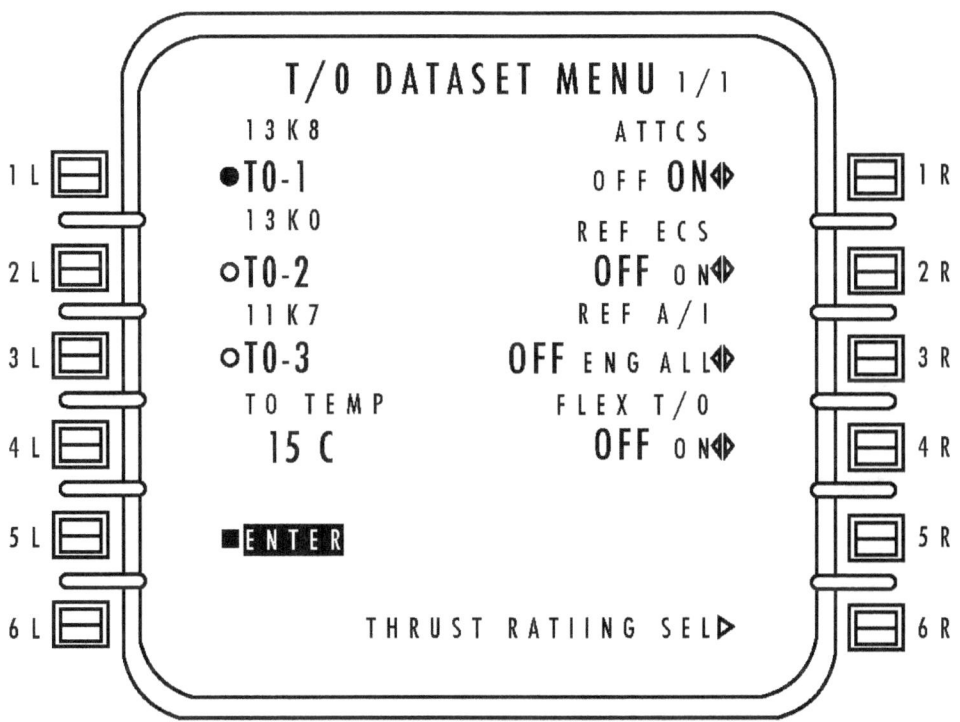

the ATTCS, ECS, anti- icing, and flex temperature are selected.

Once the inverse video ENTER is pressed the selected parameters will calculate takeoff N_1 Thrust and display that value above the N_1 icons on the EICAS. If the TO temperature value is later changed, the FLEX TO will revert to off.

The takeoff thrust is also displayed above each de- rate in pounds at sea level.

03_

PROGRESS DISPLAY

There are three pages of flight progress that display information about the current flight's progress and shows predictions of flight related performance values, such as top of climb, top of descent, and vertical speed at top of descent.

ROUTE AND FLIGHT PLAN PAGE

In the route page pilots can enter a company stored route, a pilot created route, or build a route between any two airports.

Flight plan pages show all waypoints along a route, where route pages will display airways between fixes.

Once a route is activated, ACTIVE is displayed at the top of the menu. Once either pilot modifies the route, or flight plan page the title MOD FLT PLAN is displayed at the top of the display. Modifications to an active

flight plan will show a CANCEL at 6L and an ACTIVATE prompt at 6R.

04_

EXTERIOR

The E-Jets are low wing, conventional tail, pressurized airplanes, powered by two high bypass wing-mounted turbofan engines.

The tricycle landing gear is fully retractable with dual tires for each strut.

- Side View

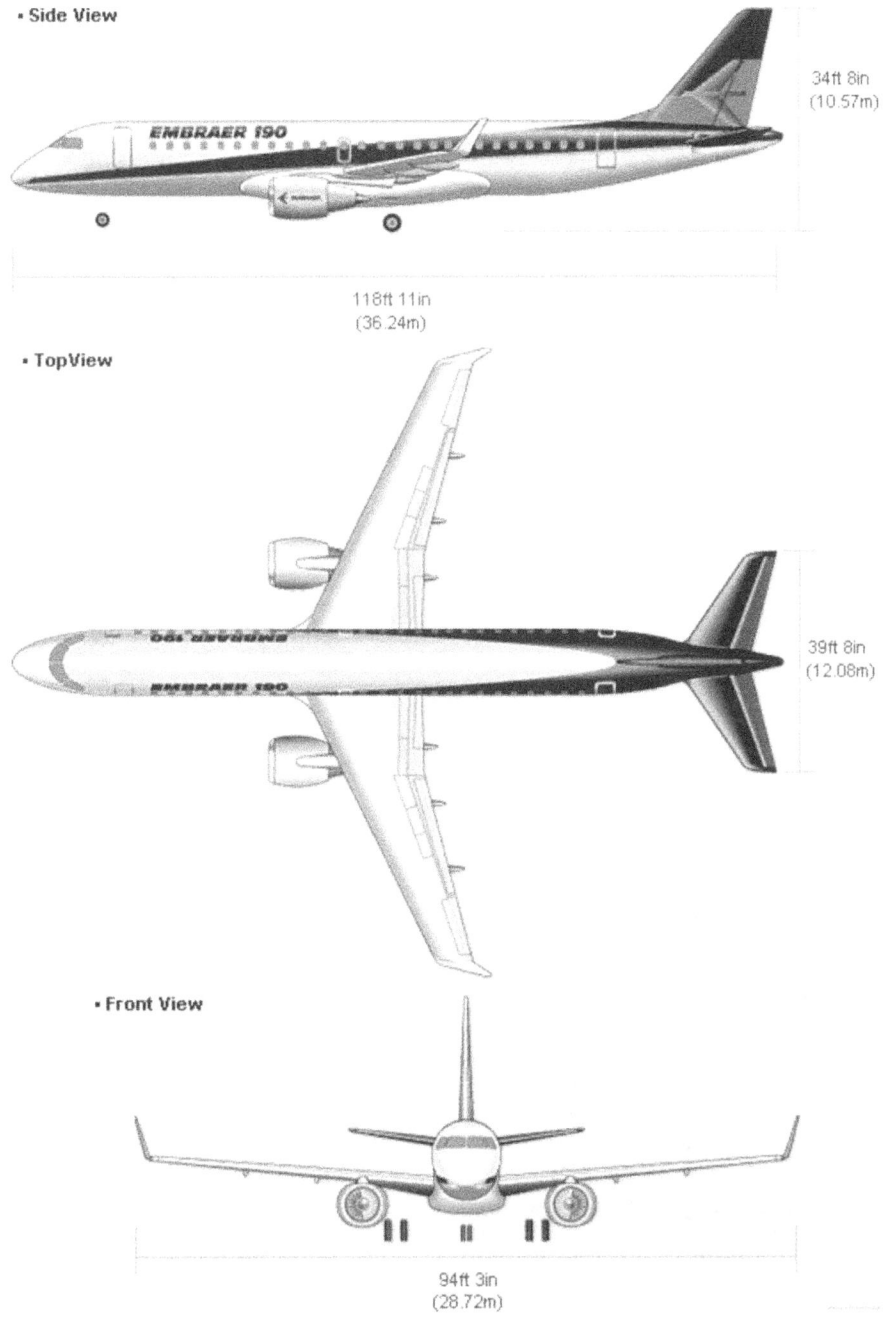

34ft 8in
(10.57m)

118ft 11in
(36.24m)

- TopView

39ft 8in
(12.08m)

- Front View

94ft 3in
(28.72m)

04_

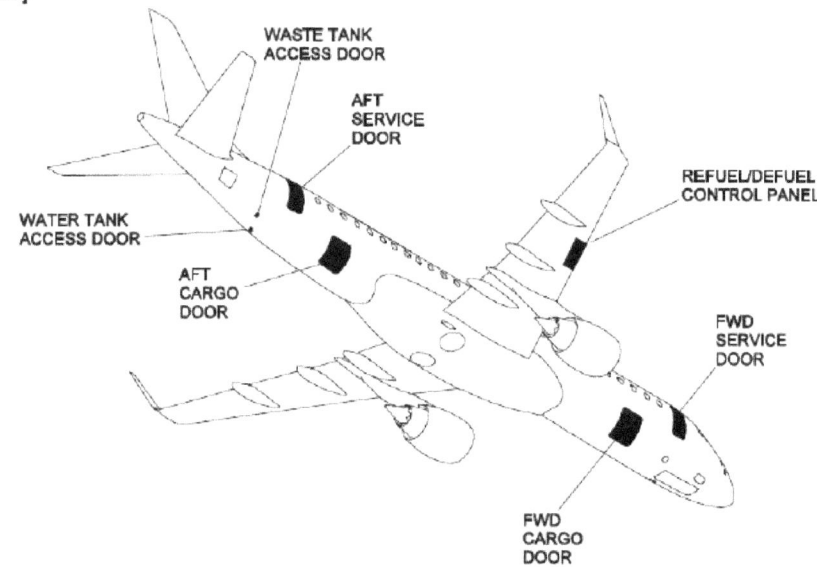

WASTE TANK
ACCESS DOOR

AFT
SERVICE
DOOR

REFUEL/DEFUEL
CONTROL PANEL

WATER TANK
ACCESS DOOR

AFT
CARGO
DOOR

FWD
SERVICE
DOOR

FWD
CARGO
DOOR

EM170AOM140536A.DGN

MAIN SERVICE POINTS

▼ GROUND SERVICE PANEL

As well as housing the external
power receptacle, crews can access
the ground power push-button,
nose wheel steering, intercom
communications and data uplink
for maintenance functions.

▼ FLAP/ SLAT SYSTEMS

The high lift control system consists of both flaps and slats on the fore and aft potions of each wing.

The slat system controls eight slat surfaces on the leading edge of the wing (four per wing) and the flap system controls four double slotted flap surfaces on the trailing edge (two per wing).

Surface position commands are given to the slat/flap actuator computer via a slat/flap control lever installed on the center pedestal in the cockpit.

04_

▼ LANDING GEAR

The nose landing gear incorporates a powered steering system, which performs the aircraft directional control on the ground.

The brake system is designed to provide manual or automatic (if applicable) airplane deceleration during ground operations.

The landing gear and brake system parameters and indications are displayed on both MFD synoptic pages. System messages are displayed on EICAS displays.

▸ SMART PROBES

The E-jets are equipped with four Air Data Smart Probes (ADSP).

The ADSP are composed of multifunction probes (pictured above) and air data computers.

The ADSP/TAT senses and transmits static pressure, total pressure, angle of attack and TAT to the Air Data System.

www.ingramcontent.com/pod-product-compliance
Lightning Source LLC
Chambersburg PA
CBHW070321290526
45791CB00003B/1198